HORMONES FROM HELL

The Ultimate Women's Humor Book

D0388750

by

JAN KING

a.k.a. The High Priestess of Progesterone

Illustrated by BOB McMAHON

CCC PUBLICATIONS • LOS ANGELES

Published by

CCC Publications
20211 Prairie Street, Suite F
Chatsworth, CA 91311

Manufactured in the United States of America

Cover design © 1990 CCC Publications

Illustrations © 1990 Jan King

Cover & interior art by Bob McMahon

Cover production by The Creative Place

ISBN: 0-918259-27-4

If your local U.S. bookstore is out of stock, copies of this book
may be obtained by mailing check or money order for $5.95 per
book (plus $2.00 to cover sales tax, postage and handling) to:
CCC Publications; 20211 Prairie Street, Suite F; Chatsworth,
CA 91311.

Pre-publication Edition — 5/90
First Printing — 9/90
Second Printing — 10/90
Third Printing — 12/90
Fourth Printing — 4/91
Fifth Printing — 6/91
Sixth Printing — 9/91

To my Mom and Dad

Betty and Frank Prahovic

With love

ACKNOWLEDGEMENT

First I would like to thank my husband and my two sons for their patience and understanding during the many hours it took to write this book. There were more times than I care to remember when they had to eat McDonald's hamburgers or pizzas for dinner. Although, they were quick to remind me that this is what I normally serve them anyway.

Next, I send my heartfelt thanks and appreciation to my publisher, Mark Chutick and my editor, Cliff Carle for their expert advice and unfailing encouragement. They were both relentless in their editing, insisting at each step that I could be funnier. So I complied, and sent them a picture of myself without my makeup on — and they finally left me alone. Thanks guys.

J.K.

CONTENTS

PREFACE

Do you remember the day when your Mom sat you down for the "Big Talk" to explain about the joys of your impending womanhood? It's one of those "special" moments in life you'll never forget. There she was — spouting off a lifetime of hormonal misinformation, while wearing her knowing womanly smile and Good Housekeeping Seal of Approval. And there we sat, in our training bras, accepting every word without reservation. Here is some of that infamous propaganda of which we have all fallen victim:

1. A young girl WELCOMES menstruation as an affirmation of her femininity.

2. There is no reason, whatsoever, for a woman to be AFRAID to go to a gynecologist.

3. A woman looks and feels her BEST during pregnancy.

4. Natural childbirth is the most BEAUTIFUL experience a woman can have.

5. Sex gets BETTER after 40.

6. Small breasts will get BIGGER with maturity.

This book is going to enlighten you enough to come out of the "hormone closet" by exploding all those stupid myths. It's also going to expose you to more female anatomy than you would find in an Adult Film Festival. Reading this book will give you new insights into what being a woman is really all about.

Raising one's consciousness above the level of one's hormones is truly an emancipating experience. You'll be able to express a new confidence in yourself and become the woman you always wanted to be: An A cup woman with a D cup attitude.

PART I
WOMEN'S
MEDICAL WOES

Chapter 1

THE GYNECOLOGY EXAM:

Taking A Deeper Look

MYTH: *There is no reason to dread going to the gynecologist.*

Oh yeah? This is THE singular event that can reduce the female of the species to a collective quivering mass of jello and send us hyperventilating into our designer paper bags. Let's examine the "little things" Mom forgot to tell us that we'll encounter during this ordeal.

STAGE #1
THE PRE-VISIT JITTERS

Women constantly shudder about the horrors in store for them as they picture themselves at the mercy of their gynecologist, Dr. Marq DeSade. Nobody wants to hear any surprise announcements from the foot of the examination table like:

"Oh-Oh, Dear. I'm afraid your kids have been punching holes in your husband's condoms again."

In order to prepare ourselves for the infliction of a number of bodily indignities, women have had to become experts in the art of self-diagnosis and self-examination. Spending months charting our temperatures for ovulation, we have been known to attend social functions with thermometers hanging out of our mouths. We have also had to perform so many breast self-exams that many of us have fallen in love with ourselves, making the art of foreplay deader than the Do-Do bird in the 20th century.

STAGE #2
THE WAITING ROOM

The second worst kept secret since Watergate is that no living gynecologist could ever be accused of punctuality. Many women have reportedly gone through menopause in the reception area while waiting to be called into the examination room. It's best to go prepared with some light reading — like the entire set of the Encyclopedia Britannica, three Leon Uris novels, and the New York Times Sunday Crossword Puzzle. This will leave you about ten minutes to spare before the nurse/receptionist/astrologer calls your name, signaling "execution" time. Keep calm and try to gain inner strength by looking at the serene expressions on the other patients' faces. However, if more than 50% of them are reading periodicals with titles such as "Malpractice Suits Made Easy" or "Do It Yourself Hysterectomies" from the Time-Life How-To Series, you might think about putting yourself in someone else's hands — like All State's.

STAGE #3
THE PRE-EXAM TESTS

As we pass through the door into the examination room, the body prepares itself for the inevitable moment of attack by a simultaneous 50 point escalation in blood pressure and by the stimulation of those powerful sweat glands which causes the sudden failure of our anti-perspirant, leaving us to wring out our dress shields. But first, we are asked to perform two impossible feats, which the

Great Houdini, had he been a woman, would have gone to the grave without mastering:

1. You must fill a urine specimen bottle possessing a .0001 millimeter neck without spillage. And since our female anatomy limits our ability to aim with the same expert marksmanship as the male of the species, you better be wearing rubber boots.

2. You must try to cover your naked body with the handkerchief-sized examining room sheet supplied.

STAGE #4
THE EXAMINATION

This is a test of pure physical survival. We are asked to lie down on a steel examination table, covered only with our 6x6 inch sheet, in a room whose temperature has never risen above 32°F. We can only hope that our Blue Cross policy contains provisions for frostbite and hypothermia.

When Dr. DeSade finally makes his guest appearance and sees your blue frozen body, he might turn to the nurse and ask:

"Are you sure this patient is still alive?"

Then he will request a recent photo of you, since this is the first and last time he'll be looking at your face. Next, you are asked to complete a series of detailed clinical questions which are necessary for a complete medical history:

1. Did you ever fail a Pap test?
    a. Did you study for it?

2. Do you always wear your diaphragm?

   a. Are you wearing it now?

3. Do you have sex with multiple partners?

   a. At the same time?

4. Does your husband always wear a condom?

   a. Does he wear it to the office?

5. Is sexual intercourse with a condom sometimes painful?

   a. Do you remove the wrapper every time?

6. Are your breasts frequently painful?

   a. Are you wearing a bra that's too small?

7. Is douching frequently painful?

   a. Do you use a jet-powered spray nozzle?

8. Have you been experiencing persistent itching?

   a. Have you tried a dandruff shampoo?

9. Would you allow a few O.B.-Gyn interns to be present in the room and watch your examination?

   a. On Donahue?

10. Do you suspect you might have a yeast infection?

    a. Are you sprouting muffins?

But don't get the wrong idea. DeSade has a lot of savoir-faire. Any doc who wears his Pap Smear Curette as a tie tac can't be all that bad. Also, all his examining tables are equipped with Gucci leather stirrups. That's class. DeSade does have two particularly annoying habits, however. One,

7

he insists on using the speculum immediately after it comes out of the hot autoclave and, two, he uses so much K-Y Jelly, his patients keep sliding off the examining table. He lies a lot, too. He always insists that the examination will not be painful. But most of us end up screaming our heads off anyway ... and this is while he is still putting on his examining glove. DeSade is not known for his gentle touch, either. When he is clumsily palpating an ovary swollen with hormonally produced follicles, he looks up to where we're plastered on the ceiling and naïvely asks: "Any pain or tenderness here?" We may find it difficult to answer distinctly because of the bullet he has placed between our teeth. It's also tough to get good medical advice from a man who's hard of hearing. Like, when asked, "How do women get fibroids?" he replies, "By eating cereals containing bran."

When at last the ordeal is over, the dextrous DeSade tries to hand us his bill, although it keeps slipping off his greased examining glove. But he's clever, I'll give him that much. He simply retrieves it by removing his tie tac curette and stabs it up off the floor. The man didn't graduate from medical school for nothing. Then he asks us to schedule another appointment for next year. Savvy in the art of Gynecological Dodging, we reply:

"Sure, put me down for December 25th."

Trying to establish a good doctor-patient relationship in any field of medicine can take a long time. The doctor should sit down with you and discuss your every concern, face to face. But since the gynecologist never gets to see your face from his end of the table, he's at a definite disadvantage here. Gynecologists are the only men on earth who are obliged to carry on all their conversations under a sheet talking directly into a cervix (with the possible exception of Rob Lowe). The only way he'll ever recognize you outside the examining room is if you're wearing your examining sheet. Therefore, every woman should take it upon herself to provide a comfortable atmosphere where she and her gynecologist can build a good rapport — invite him to your next toga party!!

Chapter 2

THE MAMMOGRAM:

Keeping Abreast
Of Technology

MYTH: *A mammogram is an easy and painless procedure.*

The first thing that should cause a great deal of alarm about the mammogram is that most of the doctors who GIVE it, can't PRONOUNCE it. A radiologist who insists on saying "mammy-o-gram" does not inspire confidence in his already nervous patients. If he can't even say it correctly, why should you entrust him with a dangerous-looking machine aimed at your chest, with the potential of creating another Chernobyl? Often, one hears a misinformed OB-Gyn recommending a "mammal-o-gram." Should we assume that this one is given at a Vet's office by a trained seal? Personally, I think the term "mammogram" is a misnomer. It sounds like somebody is going to put stamps on your breasts and mail them somewhere.

The best time to schedule a mammogram is at the completion of your monthly cycle, when your breast tissue is the least swollen from hormonal influence. Or better yet, schedule it at the completion of the hospital's monthly billing cycle, giving your bank account an extra 30 days to swell up. One hundred bucks is a pretty steep price to pay for a grotesque photo that's never going to make it into your family album.

The basic thing to remember when having your first mammogram is not to take the doctor's instructions too literally. When you are led into the freezing cubicle and asked to remove everything from the waist up, some women comply by removing their false teeth, too. You'll need to keep these as an added safety precaution — 30 minutes later, when the nurse tries to locate you, the loud chattering will act as a homing device. This leads us to the question we all want answered. Why is it that no matter what the temperature is outside, a doctor's office always remains at a constant temperature approximating that of the Arctic Circle? Do all these guys get off on the sight of gooseflesh? Or maybe it's just a good excuse for them to wear those surgical gloves all the time. With all the malpractice suits going on nowadays, perhaps they are just being careful not to leave their fingerprints on anything.

After being located, you are led down the hall and placed at the foot of a formidable looking mammography machine. Like a lamb at the sacrificial altar, you must lay out your bosom on a cold metal collection plate. If you happen to be overly endowed, the technician may have to lift up your breast and place it there FOR you — a task which she performs with the same enthusiasm as picking up a dead rat. Worse yet, if your breasts are of the AAA cup variety, a sadistic technician might make a big deal out of looking for them, even though they are ON THE TABLE. After everything is positioned properly, an upper plate comes down, looking suspiciously like a mangler from the dry cleaners. Then ... SQUISH ... those poor bazooms are flattened out until they look like two fried eggs on a skillet. The only thing which keeps the patient from fainting dead away to the floor is the fact that the monster machine has your breasts in a vise which permits a swoon of only an A or B cup latitude. In order to reposition the squashed breasts for the next picture, a technician will often enlist the aid of a pancake turner and expertly flip them off the table. For the side shot, each breast is compressed into the same thickness as a well-worn dime before they are zapped with yet more penetrating rads.

At this point, the thought will cross your mind that the next X-ray position might be upside down on your head with your breasts flopping down over your shoulders. If the incidence of brain hemorrhage weren't so high, you can be sure it would routinely be done this way.

Although we are constantly being reassured that this is a totally "harmless" procedure, the question that must be addressed is: If it's so safe, why is the doctor wearing a lead apron and operating the machine from behind a six foot concrete wall? One thing is for sure, though — if he's wearing a radiation badge that says "Over 7 Million Served", it's time to make a quick exit. We don't want to entrust our safety to a recent graduate of the McDonald's Academy of Radiation and Burger Technology where they're taught to deep-fry everything. And when you get home, if your husband remarks that you have a real "glow" about you it could mean you got an overdose. However, the resourceful woman will learn to use herself creatively in the bedroom, where she can now "light up" her sex life.

At last it's over and we sit, clutching our aching and bruised bosom, awaiting the results of our adorable "first photos." Thank goodness the equipment in most X-ray departments has become so technologically advanced, they no longer need to Fed Ex the negatives over to the PhotoMart. In the past, far too many of the male employees developed our breast photos and indiscriminately passed them around the room. Some of the sleazier help even nailed them on their bedroom walls. But now the radiographs are processed right in the hospital, and you'll get the results in less than 15 minutes ... which is just enough time for the Triple Strength Anacin to take effect so you can put your bra back on without screaming.

Holding your photos up against the light box, the doctor happily announces that all is fine in "mammy-land" — although you'd never know it from the sight of those X-rays. They look like a road map drawn by a cartographer who has spent the afternoon inhaling nitrous oxide gas. However, the radiologist is a skilled professional, adept at reading these "breast maps". He will be happy to report that your breasts look flatter than an interstate, have no visible potholes, and would be of no concern to the average road crew.

* * *

Why is it that we women are constantly put in the position of entrusting our most sacred body parts to *men* operating lethal machines? Have we learned nothing from Three Mile Island? What if the guy pushing the button turns out to be the last guy you dumped? Or what if the technician's only experience up until now has been X-raying luggage at the airport? Worse yet, how would you feel if you recognized the young man positioning your breasts in the machine from the TV show, "America's Most Wanted?"

I'm telling you, we women should get smart and start practicing "safe radiation." You never know where your last technician has been. We don't want to become "nuclear accidents waiting to happen." To insure the survival of our species, we better start sending more women to work for medical agencies instead of modeling agencies.

"IN MY PROFESSIONAL OPINION, MRS. JOHNSON,
WE SHOULD BEGIN CUTTING BACK ON YOUR
HORMONE DOSAGE."

Chapter 3

HORMONE THERAPY:

A Hair-Raising Experience

MYTH: *The doctor can clear THAT up with hormone shots.*

No matter what the ailment — warts, migraine, irritable bowel, too little or too much libido — physicians delight in prescribing the same course of treatment for all: hormone shots. What they seem to ignore is that they are fooling around with substances capable of producing awesome changes in the female body. It's a little known fact that the legendary Amazon race of women were really Pygmies being treated with progesterone. Take, for another example, one of literature's most popular characters, Dr. Jekyll/Mr. Hyde. It can now be theorized in the light of modern medical knowledge that Jekyll and Hyde were in fact, ONE MENOPAUSAL WOMAN, who was undergoing hormone therapy. The Jekyll personality was the product of a normal balance of the hormones estrogen and progesterone, responsible for regulating the complex process of ovulation and our secondary female sexual characteristics. Both hormones also directly affect our mood swings, and, when in balance will produce a relatively stable personality as seen in the Jekyll phase. However, when this phase was followed by a sudden decrease in estrogen production, the monstrous Hyde personality emerged. This personality was characterized by an increase in hair growth (especially from facial moles), violent outbursts, and a super-advanced case of generalized bitchiness.

The initial five day onslaught of estrogens catapulted her into a frenzied manic state. And all because the pharmacist misread the doctor's *Universally Bad Handwriting* on the prescription and gave her a kilogram instead of the safe milligram dosage. During that ensuing period, she cleaned every inch of her house with a grout brush, ran five simultaneous carpools, cooked 30 gourmet meals, had sex twice a day — WITH and WITHOUT her husband, and managed to find a cure for ALL Major Diseases in her full time medical practice. However, the next five days sent her on the downward spiral into a Progesterone Crisis, synthetically producing the World's Worst Case of PMS. She began to experience bloating, grew a mustache, developed fangs from a calcium imbalance, and exhibited homicidal tendencies towards her husband when he suggested they make love on Saturday night without the help of their leather marital aids.

A similar event has been chronicled in the "Three Faces of Eve" case history documenting the behavior of a woman who exhibited three separate and distinct personalities, each unaware of the presence of the others. Women agree that it's a joke to write this up in the medical journals as a *rare* occurrence, because it happens to us all, routinely, throughout the month. The PMS phase produces our weepy, hypersensitive "Slobbering Woman" personality who cries over things of monumental importance like watching our favorite defendant lose on "People's Court" or sinking into abject depression when we flunk the Jif Peanut Butter Test at the supermarket. Several days later when estrogen production hits it's peak during menstruation, the "Crazed Woman" emerges with her bizarre behavior, embarrassing the entire family. Will your kids ever forgive you for running out on the Little League field and throttling their coach over one bad call he made against their team? Thank goodness for the period of relative calm when the "Sane

Woman" shows up and takes the blame for the antics of the other two. In severe cases involving the production of more arcane hormones such as the prostaglandins, ACTH, LSH, STP, and MIT, several hundred personalities may emerge over a period of many years. Fortunately, husbands usually have no difficulty coping with this condition, because they find it exciting to sleep with a "different woman" every couple of days.

We are only now beginning to understand just how broadly hormones influence female behavior. In the latest of a string of bizarre malpractice suits reported in the *National Medical Enquirer,* a doctor from Armonk, New York, is being sued by his patient who also happens to be a Carmelite nun. As a result of an overdose of hormone shots, she was transformed from a shy and pious woman of the cloth into a sex starved vixen, dressed in gold lamé and marketing herself as "Convent Connie." She has been reportedly witnessed prowling the city streets, soliciting her "Johns-the Baptist" and promising them a real "religious experience" for ten bucks. And from all reports, she's been the answer to a lot of prayers out there.

So use caution whenever you are taking hormones of any kind. And don't forget what happened to Ann-Margret. One day, she appears as a sweet, angelic-faced Swedish maiden, singing inspirational songs on the Ed Sullivan Show — the next — she's starring in "Kitten With A Whip," clad in a skin-tight, black leather push-up bra exposing her pulsating bosom, while straddling the vibrating, stud-covered leather seat on her boyfriend's Harley-Davidson. Stories of estrogen abuse are a dime a dozen in Hollywood. And any starlet who "does estrogen" risks suffering permanent brain damage from being bounced around in all those hard-core jiggle movies.

Recently, doctors have been prescribing male hormones, such as testosterone, to alleviate some of the troublesome side effects of heavy menstrual cycles. But little has been reported about its worst side effect: heart attack — her husband's, when he wakes up next to a wife sporting a *bushy mustache* and an advanced case of *5 o'clock shadow*.

The problem of nationwide hormone abuse has become epidemic as demonstrated by the increasing size and number of "busts" in this country. In fact, the U.S. Government under the current administration has made it a top priority by creating a Hormone Regulatory Board which has issued guidelines covering all controlled hormonal substances. It would require convicted hormone abusers to do several months of hard time on "Geraldo" and "A Current Affair." The prescribing physician would be given a life sentence behind bars at a maximum security Hormonal Detention Center policed by pre-menopausal Nazi matrons. Here he would be forced to wear the standard prison issue of an 18 hour girdle, high heels, and a Zsa Zsa wig, while wet nursing the matron's offspring. And if this isn't torture enough, he could be ordered to share not only the Zsa Zsa wig, but also the same cell with Zsa Zsa herself! This would finally bring him face to face with a hormone atrocity he helped to create and will, no doubt, shock him into going straight.

PART I QUIZ

1. The ovaries play a major role in:
   - a. the latest Cher video
   - b. divorce proceedings
   - c. Flaubert's "Madame B. Ovary"
   - d. Wayne Newton's singing career

   *d (they were also instrumental in his reaching puberty)

2. Never patronize a gynecologist who:
   - a. wears larger than a size 5 glove
   - b. skimps on the K-Y jelly
   - c. mistakes his shoe tree for the speculum
   - d. allows 15 pre-med students in the room to observe

   *all of the above (and in the same order of importance)

3. It is essential to see your gynecologist:
   - a. before the 9th month of pregnancy
   - b. moonlighting at Chippendales
   - c. away from the office if he is handsome
   - d. while keeping both of his feet on the floor

   *d (unless b and c are true)

4. Never enter a gynecologist's examining room:
   - a. wearing something from Victoria's Secret
   - b. without first knocking — if his nurse is in with him
   - c. backwards
   - d. where a video camera is operating

   *d (unless you are showing your best angle)

5. A mammogram can't be given:

    a. while wearing your lead-lined support bra
    b. on a date
    c. by a certified public accountant
    d. in Braille

    *c (although countless CPAs will insist they are qualified)

6. You'll know your mammogram was done incorrectly if:

    a. your breasts glow at night
    b. the X-Rays show kidney stones
    c. the technician's radiation badge melts
    d. the rabbit dies

    *b (who knows where they'll try to insert the catheter)

7. Which facility would be most suitable for a mammogram:

    a. Three Mile Island Community Hospital
    b. The Columbia School of Broadcasting
    c. Dave's Pleasure Palace
    d. Bob-the-Producer's casting couch

    *(they all check out okay with our sources)

8. Do not allow a radiologist to perform a mammography if his badge:

    a. says New York Cab Driver #443564
    b. says Over 3 Billion Served
    c. has recently stopped a bullet
    d. says Troop 43 B.S.A.

    *a (especially if his meter is running)

9. A hormone is considered too potent if you wake up with:
   a. gonads
   b. a beard
   c. 6 neighborhood men
   d. a wolf pack

   *b (the others are easier to keep secret)

10. A woman who is taking male hormones might appear to be:
    a. well-hung
    b. her husband from a distance
    c. Arnold Schwarzenegger in drag
    d. none of the above

    *d (Schwarzenegger looks puny by comparison)

11. Prostaglandins are manufactured by:
    a. way of a miracle in transsexuals
    b. Beatrice
    c. Wham-O
    d. the U.S. Government

    *b (Beatrice owns a, c and d)

12. How do you make a hormone:
    a. with synthetic steroids
    b. with amino acids
    c. in a government approved facility
    d. don't pay her

    *d (and you were just waiting for this answer, weren't you?)

PART II

CRIMES OF PROGESTERONE: A LIFE SENTENCE

"LET ME GUESS — COULD IT BE NEARING
THAT TIME OF THE MONTH?"

Chapter 4

P.M.S.

or Pardon My Screaming

MYTH: *PMS is all in your head.*

That myth is a thing of the past. PMS is no longer a psychological condition to be treated as lightly as Scarlett and her "vapors." We're talking about the power of hormones here. And they can change you from a passive Donna Reed into a cop-slugging Zsa Zsa before you can say "plea bargain." There is even a new judicial ruling which states that PMS can be grounds for justifiable homicide. Even Rusty the Bailiff on "People's Court" is packing heat on estrogen related cases. So husbands better think twice about coming home and making broad statements like this one to a PMS indisposed spouse: "So — all you did was stay home and clean the house today?"

This man has uttered the last stupid statement he will ever make. Just read the tabloid headlines touting the aftermath:

MAN STRANGLED TO DEATH BY WIFE USING UNDERWIRE BRA AS LETHAL WEAPON! — Wife pleads PMS induced temporary insanity. Jury of 12 pre-menopausal women votes for acquittal.

So the next time you try "getting off" with a woman suffering from PMS, you had better think twice. The only thing you're likely to *get* is a knife in the heart! Then she'll be the one *getting off* — with only a slap on the wrist from the judge.

It's not bad enough that women suffer through their monthly period, itself, but we also have to contend with being water logged for two weeks beforehand. Most of us have taken to wearing bell-bottom panty hose to accommodate our hormonally swollen ankles. Water retention makes us irritable, achy, tense, and even in some cases, disoriented. And doctors insist that it's "all in our heads." If they really believe that, then they also must expect to find our brains located in our pelvis.

Water retention is also the culprit in an unsightly condition known as "pitting edema." You know you've got it when you wake up one morning, mid-month, and see body tissue that has metamorphosized overnight into the same texture as the Pillsbury Doughboy. We watch in fascinated revulsion as our thighs develop dents every time we poke them with our finger. Poke ... dent ... poke ... dent ... poke ... dent ... along each leg until they begin to look, alarmingly, more and more like a relief map of the surface of the moon. The only time you'll see craters bigger than these are on the faces of test cases for Retin-A. By the time you poke your way down toward your feet, each ankle appears to be developing a goiter. This definitely rules out wearing those smart ankle strap shoes for the rest of the month. Those ankles could only be supported by the black orthopedic shoes last seen on the feet of all the nuns at Our Lady of

Buster Brown Convent. Yes, PMS makes a bad fashion statement, ladies!

Unfortunately, the water retention is not only confined to our legs. There is also the little-talked-about breast tenderness-cum-agony condition that makes it impossible to sleep on your stomach or hug your child without experiencing gut wrenching pain. It can be very traumatic for a child to have the comfort of being held to his mother's bosom interrupted by her constant screams. Plus, an engorged breast can inflict a mean brain contusion that could keep your kid reading Dr. Seuss for the rest of his natural life. It can add a sour note to lovemaking, too — especially when your husband reaches out in his most amorous mood only to hear:

"You touch me THERE, buddy, and I'll rip your face off!"

This does not exactly do a lot to enhance romance in the bedroom. And don't overlook the fact that hormonally engorged mammary tissue can pose a serious threat. Just the act of taking off your bra too quickly could result in a nasty whiplash!

Husbands ought to learn from the kids in the family. They intuitively understand the plight of their Moms. When asked to draw their Mommies, most first graders depicted them as a watermelon with legs sloshing around the kitchen. Others astutely drew them with two heads, one bearing the smiley face and the other not only having the smile inverted but with daggers sticking out of its eyes.

All I can say is that women are getting pretty sick of this menstrual thing. And we're holding our hormones accountable. For two weeks you're pre-menstrual, then for a week you're menstrual, then for another two weeks you're post-menstrual ... hey — if we have five good minutes a month, it's a miracle!!

Chapter 5

P.M.P.

or Pardon My Period

MYTH: *A young girl should welcome menstruation as an ongoing affirmation of her femininity.*

This is one of those "touchy" topics you would think is just too personal to talk about. There are some things we just don't need to know about each other, and menstrual flow could be at the top of that list! Although it might surprise most men that when women get together, it's usually discussed to the exclusion of all else, even sex. Women unanimously agree their grandmothers had the right idea when they described it as "The Curse", or when the girls in the locker room called it "That Filthy Time of the Month". Or perhaps the most colorful of all comes from the male population, who have always referred to it as "Having the Rag On." We often wonder just who was the *Original Airhead* responsible for perpetrating such insipid phrases as "Feminine Fulfillment" and "Having Her Special Days." Show us one woman who even remotely enjoys having a period, and we'll show **you a woman who equally enjoys getting razor nicks.**

Worse yet, is the woman who seeks a certain amount of celebrity through her period — like Cathy Rigby. Just hope and pray she never comes to your house, smiling away as she totes that giant box of sanitary pads for her overnight stay. If this gal has to use that many pads in 24 hours, she needs to have a D & C.

Menstruation is one of nature's most fickle hormonal functions which chooses the most inopportune times to appear, sabotaging your every chance to enjoy life. Why bother to keep a calendar charting the dates of your expected periods when you KNOW they will always appear:

1. In a restaurant while wearing your best white silk dress.

2. On your honeymoon. Often, this occurs because your father has prayed so hard for it to happen this way.

3. On vacation. Going to Hawaii? Don't even bother to pack your bathing suit. A Vuitton trunk full of tampons will suffice.

4. On an airplane. This is most likely the result of the toxic airline food directly poisoning the uterus, causing severe contractions, which then compels you to spend most of your flight in the plane's bathroom. Once in there, take advantage of the giant sanitary pads they offer — they're as big as a 747 and have their own installation crew.

5. Any time you're not carrying a tampon in your purse. So be prepared for the unexpected, like Karl Malden is — and "Don't leave home without it."

6. When visiting an old folk's home. Another of Mother Nature's sadistic tricks, this is the one place where a tampon hasn't been SEEN much less USED by anyone since Bess Truman left the White House.

Some enterprising company could make billions if they figured out how to design a tampon that didn't leak. Trying to beat this problem, women spend uncharted hours in their bathrooms positioning these things at every angle imaginable. Some even risk having to undergo emergency episiotomies by inserting them in multiples, in an attempt to "beat the leak." Still, most tampons can't go for more than an hour without developing stress fractures, especially on the first day of your period. That's the day your estrogen is racing faster than anything clocked at Daytona.

* * *

Next, we have to address the issue of all those controversial hysterectomies performed soon after the age of 40. You'll have to decide if you would rather be "half a woman" who's out there vigorously enjoying life or a whole one with a hematocrit so low you're too weak to tie your sneakers. And is the only other method of escaping "having it" by "not having it" — via a nine month pregnancy? Some choice! It's like asking you to choose between the electric chair and the gas chamber. Menopause is looking better and better every day, gals. We can't wait for the days of toilets unclogged from plastic applicators! White undies! Purses not cluttered with minis, maxis, and mega pads! And last but not least — the simple act of walking erect instead of being doubled over with cramps!

And speaking of cramps ... It's not considered hip to get busted for Midol abuse on "those" days. But what's a woman to do? Those enduring a body ravaged by cramps have taken to the practice of speedballing Midol and Motrin for allegedly fast ... fast ... fast relief. The only other alternative is to become surgically joined at the abdomen to a hot water bottle.

* * *

In the past five years, it seems like doctors have been discovering new female hormones at the rate of about one per week. One fatty acid complex, fingered as being responsible for a lot of menstrual irregularities, is called prostaglandins. Now this is one ugly word. It sounds like something the male prostate gland should be producing if it's working properly. I don't know about you, but I'd be just as happy not knowing about a lot of these hormones. Suppose you produce too much of this prostaglandin stuff. Does this mean women will have to go through those same awful exams men get where they're asked to cough? One rubber glove exam is quite enough for us, thank you.

Another hormone referred to as FSH, or follicle stimulating hormone, is responsible for manufacturing a chemical which stimulates *follicle production* in the ovaries. Doesn't this sound like something you'd give to a bald guy? Then there's LH, or leutinizing hormone. Nobody is quite sure about its function, except some believe it's used in that process which polishes and shines automobile bodies.

One thing is for sure, gals. A lot more of us need to start living our lives for the moment. With all these unstable chemicals floating around inside us, it's only a matter of time before they combine with the plastic in the women with *boob jobs,* and cause spontaneous detonation.

Chapter 6

P.M.I.

or Pardon My Incontinence

MYTH: *Life begins after 40.*

That's what we've been told. Our time will finally come to ditch the kids, and spend our days clad in an elegant Katherine Hepburn silk pantsuit, blissfully rowing around on Golden Pond. The Blue Haired Cocktail Hour of Life was meant to be enjoyed in brimming good health, with unbridled energy, and a true sense of *joie de vivre*. This is the picture we have painted and thought would be ours — until lately. Now all we have to do is flip the channels on TV and find any number of highly respected actresses doing commercials which tell us that by age 50, our rapidly decreasing hormone levels will cause the abrupt deterioration of all our bodily functions. But not to worry. They also just happen to represent the manufacturers of the miraculous pharmaceutical products which will help us cope with those conditions responsible for our inevitable decline into Hygienic Senility:

INCONTINENCE

What a major gross out to watch perky little June Allyson extolling the virtues of Depends, the Pampers of the Geriatric Set. According to June, at no time in history have so many had so little control. It's enough to make us all get on the floor and do 50 compulsory Kegel exercises a day.

DENTURE ODOR

As if June wasn't bad enough, we also must heed the warnings from the legendary Martha Raye. Now, besides having bladders with less muscle tone than Pee Wee Herman's biceps, we could be suffering from embarrassing denture stains and odor, too. Come on, Martha — stains and odor? Are we talking DOGS or DENTURES here?

DENTAL PLATE MISCARRIAGES

These ads usually feature some gray haired old woman giving testimony as to how her upper plate fell out while eating corn-on-the-cob at the family reunion. Not a flattering portrait. But worse is the notion that, past 50, if we indulge in any hearty laughter, we are in danger of losing our water AND our teeth at the same time! But trying to choke back all that laughter puts an awfully tough strain on the belly. That's why all those old people wear hernia trusses.

HEMORRHOIDS

The only TV scenario which could possibly be MORE offensive would be one in which Helen Hayes is introduced as the First Lady of the American Theatre, Tony Award winner, and HEMORR-HOID SUFFERER. Why are the commercials for this thoroughly humiliating subject always aired during "prime time" and with older and pregnant women as "prime targets?" Women have always fought the image of being referred to as "a big pain in the butt." We do not want ourselves filmed in public places such as restaurants, churches, and art galleries discussing our symptomatic pain, itch, and swelling in alarming detail to prove it. So we can either suffer this fate, or we can take their advice — use Preparation H and "Kiss Those Hemorrhoids Goodbye." (Not with *these* lips!)

CONSTIPATION

Why do these commercials center all their attention on the state of an elderly woman's bowels? Would you want to represent your species by being handed the Clio Award for the best dramatic actress in the following commercial presentation? You're playing the part of a pathetic old woman, dressed in a K-Mart robe and scuffies, moping around your daughter's house in such a state of bowel induced lethargy, you can barely walk. Your hotshot daughter appears on the scene, shaking her head in disgust and says, "Mom — you need help — big time. Here's the Family Friend." At which point she whips out a box of laxatives bigger than Economy Size Tide. Oh spare us!

FEMININE ODOR

The ultimate insult to the mature woman is delivered by a daughter who lectures her ignorant mother about the beneficial effects of douching away odor-causing bacteria. The killing blow is leveled when her daughter hands her the bottle of douching compound and says with a sly smile: "I chose the Springtime Regular formula, and I bought the Double Industrial Strength for you." Well thanks a lot, hon. I guess you knew a real woman could take it.

FEMININE ITCHING

Cleverly handling this delicate subject, the advertiser creates a strong association with femininity as we watch an elegant woman dressed in a satin peignoir, sitting at her dressing table brushing her hair. The camera pans in on a close-up of the feminine itching spray atop of milady's vanity surrounded by wildflowers, lace doilies, and pearls. However, if this was done as a documentary, the camera would catch both the woman and her dog rolling around on the floor in abject misery scratching like there was no tomorrow. The truth is that they would probably both feel a lot better after a good flea dip.

OSTEOPOROSIS

This condition was discovered and named for Drs. Porosis and Osteo in a remote village in Prague. They noticed that the declining production of estrogen in women past 50 was leeching away the calcium in their bones until they possessed less strength than that of the average hummingbird ... not to mention the posture of Quasimodo. If left untreated, all of the female species, 60 years old or above, would be eligible to be scientifically classified as Invertebrates. How low does that make you feel?

* * *

Well, ladies — you don't have to be Einstein to figure out that our hormones are doing us in. While we've still got them, they're raising hell with every bodily function going on in us, and when we lose them, the situation becomes worse. Forget Golden Pond. We're probably going to meet the fate of being put out to pasture along with a

bunch of burned-out old stud horses. By the way
... They shoot horses, don't they?

PART II QUIZ

1. Ten days prior to your period, the size of your belly has swollen to basketball proportions. This is due to:

   a. an immaculate conception
   b. the Dr. J Syndrome
   c. a fast slam dunk
   d. the dangerous fad of helium sniffing

   *a (if your weight gain is about 9 lbs. 5 oz.)

2. Your legs are exhibiting the effects of "pitting edema." You should avoid:

   a. olives
   b. salt licks
   c. kinky sex
   d. pole vaulting

   *c & d (done at the same time results in automatic disqualification by the judges)

3. Breast tenderness can be linked to:

   a. excessive handling
   b. Merry Widow bras
   c. a dry cleaner who uses too much starch
   d. Glasnost

   *d (which is a newly-devised Soviet hormonal plot)

4. During your child's school play, you break into hysterical sobbing. This behavior is:
   a. a result of his embarrassing performance
   b. an average PMS reaction
   c. normal — if the play lasts more than 4 hours
   d. approved by the Board of Education

   *d (most Boards of Education suffer from mass PMS)

5. Estrogen and progesterone are secreted by:
   a. the CIA
   b. Michael Jackson and Prince
   c. a well-oiled uterus
   d. the Bush Administration

   *c (when it is serviced regularly by Mr. Goodwrench)

6. Women who love getting their periods are:
   a. probably anemic
   b. called masochists
   c. mental patients
   d. tampon abusers

   *d (and are usually jailed without parole until menopause)

7. It's best to remove a tampon:
   a. using the Heimlich Maneuver
   b. when your labor pains are about 3 minutes apart
   c. when the weight forces you to your knees
   d. if the neighborhood cats are following you around

   *a (it's the fastest and neatest method to date)

8. The new sanitary pads with "wings" absorb more — AND:
    a. contain a powerful decongestant
    b. tickle your fancy
    c. stick to your underpants but not to your dentures
    d. need "clearance" before they can be taken off

    * none of the above (they become airborne before you can use them)

9. A modern aid to the problem of incontinence is:
    a. a beach towel
    b. a porta-john
    c. a bucket
    d. June Allyson

    *d (June's got it by a nose — or, in this case, a bladder)

10. A hemorrhoidal suppository may be necessary when:
    a. the hemorrhoids exceed the size of the Alps
    b. you have to drive your car standing up
    c. you're trying to kick the cigarette habit
    d. the sore throat persists for more than 3 days

    *a (your first clue is a Rand/McNally survey crew arriving at your door.)

11. What can be done about embarrassing feminine odor:

    a. blame it on your dog
    b. marry a bum and "stand by your man"
    c. stand by your can (trash or garbage)
    d. switch to tartar control Crest

    *b or c (and if they don't work, stand well down wind)

12. The practice of douching may:

    a. require a license
    b. become habit forming
    c. also be called a royal flush
    d. reduce cavities

    *c (which automatically makes you Queen For A Day)

PART III

THE PERILS OF PREGNANCY

"UH, OH … THIS IS DEFINITELY GOING
TO BE A TOUGH DELIVERY."

Chapter 7

NATURAL CHILDBIRTH:

A Pain In The Butt

(or somewhere in that vicinity)

MYTH: *Natural childbirth is the most beautiful experience a woman can have.*

This chapter is going to tell a little story. A story about natural childbirth. Can you spell natural childbirth? Women can. It's spelled:

A-G-O-N-Y

You can forget all that hype about natural childbirth being the most "beautiful" experience of your life. If this is true, ladies, then we haven't got much to live for. Although, it could be argued that the pain of childbirth prepares you for the agony of being a parent.

Every woman has a childbirth story to tell. The trouble is most of them were delirious from the anesthesia, so they can't recall what really happened. Listen to me, the High Priestess of Progesterone, because I'm going to give it to you straight — a step by step, contraction by contraction, pant-blow by pant-blow account from my own experience:

We were expecting our second child, and I was going to have no part of the old-fashioned unconscious delivery. No sir. Just good old gut-wrenching pain for me, to prove how worthy I was to wear the Badge of Motherhood. Okay, I lied already. I will admit to being a teeny bit reluctant to the idea of delivering with no anesthesia. So I casually remarked to my O.B. one day while I was down on bended knees:

"Could you give me a spinal — please, please, oh pretty please? ... No? ... Okay, okay then ... how about twilight sleep? Demerol? Anesthetically induced coma?"

But he refused, citing the 49th Medical Ethics Amendment — something about not wanting to deny the patient's constitutional right to Pain and Suffering. So I was dragged, kicking and screaming, to the LaMaze classes. They were filled with zombie-like Yuppie couples who wore a fixed smile on their faces and chanted foreign expressions like "pain threshold" and "parental bonding."

The nurse instructor demonstrated the art of "breathing" in every way known to Eastern Religion. There were cleansing breaths, relaxation breaths, and shallow breaths. However, no one mentioned the kind that accompanies the last stage of labor — bad breath. And let's face it. There's no one on hand to pass you the Listerine in the labor room. Breathing techniques supposedly ease the various stages of "discomfort" during labor. The instructors are very careful to never utter the word p-a-i-n. That would be a grievous breach of the basic LaMaze philosophy: If these women have any idea of what's REALLY going to happen, the organization's dead.

Then one day in my ninth month, I awoke to find our water bed had sprung a leak — except we didn't own one. We called the doctor, who promised he would meet us in the emergency room immediately. True to his Hippocratic Oath, he showed up two hours and six towels later. So they dragged me, soggy bottom and all, onto the examining table for a look. When the doctor inserted the speculum, I heard a whoosh of tidal wave proportions after which he announced the brilliant clinical diagnosis: "We need a mop in here."

I was wheeled up to the labor room where they were going to attempt "inducing" labor. Who would have guessed that the medical definition of "induce" is ENEMA? No one mentioned this in LaMaze class. So I was given an enema plus a suppository to stimulate labor. Actually, from the way it felt, it would be more accurate to say it was given to "simulate" labor. The power of an explosive bowel on top of being nine months pregnant is enough to deliver quadruplets. Next, my O.B. ordered a "Pit Drip." This "meaningful" experience consists of running an IV loaded with the lethal hormone pitocin into the veins, producing uterine contractions of roughly the same pain intensity as an attack from a "Pit Bull". Imagine Hulk Hogan bouncing on your stomach for three hours non-stop. Now you've got the picture!

Whatever happened to those wonderful cleansing and relaxing breaths? No time to put THEM into practice when labor comes on this hard and fast. Just when I thought I'd pass out from the pain, the doctor decided this was the ideal time for another pelvic exam. The further bodily insult of a rubber glove during this crescendo of pain felt like someone was trying to park a Mack Truck in my garage built for a Volkswagen. But who was I to start screeching and spoil the event that everyone promised would be one of the most "beautiful experiences" of my life?

Next, the labor nurse astutely brought to my attention that I was in "transition — the toughest part of labor." Oh yeah. I was sure glad she pointed it out to me, otherwise I might not have noticed that my body felt like it was trying to pass a kidney stone the size of Gibraltar.

"Tough?" I screamed. "And up till now it's just been dress rehearsal?"

"I know, dear. But let's do our pant-blow breathing."

"YOU do the pant-blow breathing. I'm just gonna lie here and scream till I rupture a vocal chord."

The labor room I shared along with three other women had all the ambience of a snake pit. There was more screaming going on in there than in all the "Friday the 13th" movies combined. And most of it came from the doctor, when he realized our lengthy labors were going to cause him to miss Monday Night Football.

To my amazement, the pain suddenly stopped — only to be followed by another more horrifying sensation called "pushing." The pushing sensation is an entirely primal experience. It can only be described as feeling like trying to expel the New York Giants football team. After awhile, when you're half dead from exhaustion, they tell you NOT to push anymore. This is like trying to hold back Moby Dick plus the ocean he's swimming in. So I crossed my legs and prayed while being wheeled into the delivery room.

The next thing I remember was a voice from God saying: "Would you like some anesthesia now?"

The instant the mask hit my face, I began sucking in the anesthesia faster than Pavarotti can ingest pasta. Then the world turned pink and started to spin. I awoke in the recovery room where a burly nurse was pushing down on my belly every few minutes to insure all the afterbirth was expelled. This part, of course, was also not covered in the LaMaze class.

"Listen, Hon" I snapped at the nurse. "Why don't you just rip out my toenails one by one? It would be kinder."

To this day, I still hold great compassion for a tube of toothpaste.

After being wheeled back to my room, the nurse set up a sun lamp in a position which gave me the most bizarre suntan of my life. Between that and the alternating ice packs, my lower extremities were subjected to a range of the most extreme climatic conditions a human being will ever endure on this earth. It's no mystery to me why the dinosaurs became extinct.

The hard fact is that after delivering, the pain and discomfort do not abruptly end here. We've got all the residual *benefits* to deal with ... like hemorrhoids, episiotomy stitches, and swelling. And worse still, after delivering, every woman dreads the first time she has to go to the john. We can break out into a cold sweat just THINKING about what it's going to feel like. Let's just say that if the

56

delivery is like expelling the Giants football team, *here* we're talking the entire stadium!

It's important to know that we do have a choice, ladies. And having tried it both ways, I lay them out before you as an objective party. You can go the natural route without benefit of anesthesia and with every sense acutely heightened; experience fully every gut-wrenching nuance of pain and torture imaginable with the no-good-lousy-rotten scumbag of a man you hold responsible for your condition at your side, getting in your face with his stupid, irritating, asinine breathing instructions which he shouts out with his smelly, offensive, maggot-like breath for 30 or more non-stop pain wracking hours of labor, culminating in a tissue-tearing, organ-squeezing, bone-crushing delivery.

Or ... you can selflessly give up this "beautiful experience," by numbing your body to the intense pleasures of childbirth with an epidural.

Is there an anesthesiologist in the house?

Chapter 8

THE BODY PREGNANT:

A Lesson In Really Gross Anatomy

MYTH: *90% of the population agrees a woman looks her most BEAUTIFUL during pregnancy.*

Our answer to that ... get new glasses! What they failed to mention was that the people polled for this statement were all owners of seeing eye dogs — and the 10% negative vote was cast by the dogs. The statement that women look their most beautiful during pregnancy is made by the same kind of people who attend wakes and remark how good the corpse looks. Take it from those of us who have been there, the combination of potent hormones produced during your nine months of pregnancy creates a series of bodily mutations more bizarre than Jeff Goldblum went through in "The Fly."

It's true that a pregnant woman is always the center of attention. The nature of her changing body is a constant source of fascination to all — which is why a pregnant woman would be perfect to be cast as the lead in remakes of the following theatrical productions:

"HAIR"

One of the first changes caused by pregnancy hormones is the gross increase in hair ... or in this case ... the increase in gross-looking hair. And not the kind found on top of the head. We're talking hair growth in some mighty strange places. Long about the 3rd month, you'll wake up one morning and find a strange fuzzy black line of hair making a track up the middle of your stomach, heading towards the belly button. Your first reaction?

Scream and grab a can of Raid! But on closer inspection, you realize that it's part of YOU and it's *now* rapidly growing upward towards your chest! This look does not exactly do a lot for your sexy nighties. It tends to evoke an "Ape Woman Meets Frederick's of Hollywood" image in the eye of the beholder. And where did that mustache come from? Pass the bleach! You might want to consider gainful employment in the European film industry or Ringling Brothers at this point in your life. And no matter how diligently we work out with our razors, pregnant women can always be spotted by the telltale 5 o'clock shadow under their L'eggs.

"PHANTOM OF THE OPERA"

Another hormonally induced phenomenon called the "mask of pregnancy" can show up as early as the first trimester. It manifests itself as a darkly pigmented area in a butterfly-shaped pattern across the bridge of the nose and upper lip. So for the next six months, you better get used to people making remarks like...

"Say, Ma'am. Did you know there's a Gypsy moth nesting on your nose?"

"THE ELEPHANT MAN"

Meanwhile, as the belly continues to distend, the skin develops shiny "stretch marks" looking suspiciously like those big runners in doubleknit polyester. Functioning like road expanders, these things can end up with the same depth and tread as on a new set of Goodyears. By the sixth month, the belly accommodates its rapidly increasing volume by doing a very unorthodox thing — the belly button pops inside out. Now that's some kinky silhouette under all your maternity knits! It would defy Nature to find one "innie" left in all of Preggieland.

"LES MISERABLES"

Not to be outdone by the tummy, the breasts are manufacturing the same powerful hormones found in watermelons which cause them to swell up very rapidly. Many women find it advisable to wear the warning sign: CAUTION — CONTENTS UNDER PRESSURE to insure public safety. In most cases, you'll make Dolly look like she's wearing a training bra. In general, the pregnant breast poses two major problems:

1. Trying to sit up straight at the dinner table without pitching forward into your chicken soup.

2. When you take off your bra at night, the sensation of releasing those giant engorged boobs is like having two hot heifers plopped on your belly. And speaking of cows, you're now producing more quarts per day than a whole dairy farm.

Unfortunately, not only the front of the body pregnant undergoes an unflattering metamorphosis. From the rear, those expanding pelvic bones produce a behind whose width merits being red flagged as a "wide load."

"EXTREMITIES"

The legs really take a beating in the last trimester of pregnancy. Varicose veins the size of Ziti pop up overnight giving the illusion that you're wearing Argyle knee socks. And the added problem of fluid retention means you'll be splitting the seams on everything from pants to stockings. What's the answer? ... Double-strength *Queen Size* panty hose (i.e. big enough to fit the average *Drag Queen!*) And the sooner the better! Most women need them 24 hours after conception. In fact, most husbands come to wish their wives had been wearing them ON the night of conception.

"GREASE"

How about that "special glow" which is attributed to all pregnant women? Take a closer look. The rosy flush is nothing more than a network of spider veins surfacing like enemy submarines. And the sudden appearance of these little red veins etched all over the face should be no mystery — they're directly proportional to the length of morning sickness you experience. It's simple: The more wretching — the more etching. And nothing less than Volcanic Strength Clearasil can help clear up those huge hormonal zits which erupt with less warning than Mt. St. Helens and produce more oil than your average OPEC Nation can barrel in a day.

"STOP THE WORLD I WANT TO GET OFF"

"Morning Sickness?" — If only it was confined to the mornings! By the second month, the carpet between your bed and bathroom has acquired skid marks rivaling those at the Indy 500. In your hormonally altered state, sights and smells which you normally take for granted now become enemy stimuli causing you to toss your cookies at the drop of a hat. It can be especially distressing when you sit down to dinner at your in-laws, take one bite of your mother-in-law's prized beef stroganoff and promptly unload all over her precious lace tablecloth.

*　*　*

MYTH: *Some women's pregnancies are so unnoticeable through the first 6-8 months, nobody (including the mother herself) has any idea they are carrying a child.*

Couldn't you just gag over those old Doris Day movies in which she finds herself six months along but acts flabbergasted when the doctor gives her the news she's pregnant? Like she had no idea where two passion-filled weeks in the Motel 6 with Cary Grant would lead. Let's lose the denial thing, Doris. After gaining 54 pounds and feeling a little fist banging on the inside of your belly, most women finally admit to experiencing something a bit more profound than gas. Doris should have consulted our guidelines which take all the guesswork out of wondering whether you're pregnant or not. You ARE if you:

1. Notice that your pregnancy kit test tube has more rings around it than the planet Saturn.

2. Find yourself gagging over your cereal bowl in the morning and camping by your toilet bowl every night.

3. Are growing body hair at a rate which would give Lon Chaney a run for his money.

4. Begin wearing the same size underpants as Nell Carter. On second thought — once you reach this size, it's a dead giveaway you're ready to deliver triplets.

5. Are napping continuously from breakfast through Johnny Carson. "Unconscious" is going to pretty much describe you at your

most scintillating for the next nine months. Let's just say that the "departed one" at the funeral will look like the life of the party next to you.

* * *

After you have established your pregnancy by carefully consulting our guidelines, the next most commonly asked question is — "How will I know when it's time to go to the hospital once labor has started?" Here's some tips:

1. When your "persistent indigestion" is accompanied by contractions every three minutes.

2. Go IMMEDIATELY to the hospital when your contractions are severely interfering with your foreplay. Do not get dressed and do not collect your $100 dollars!

3. When your Nike Air's are doubling as flotation devices.

4. When you look down at your shoes and notice an extra pair of feet dangling between your own.

* * *

So, who ARE these people who keep saying that pregnancy brings out the best in a woman? Get real! If the "best" consists of varicose veins, pimples, edema, uneven pigmentation, overactive oil glands, and a protruding belly button, we're all in big trouble. Are these the standards the public sets which qualifies us as attractive pregnant women??? Kind of a warped perception, I'd say.

But then again, they all thought the crazed dame in "Fatal Attraction" was gorgeous. Going along with this kind of thinking, I guess a nine month pregnant woman would look scary enough to project the perfect image as the star in the upcoming sequel: "Fetal Attraction."

68

Chapter 9

SEX DURING PREGNANCY:

The Agony Of Defeat

MYTH: *Most doctors agree that you should continue to enjoy "normal sexual activity" throughout your pregnancy.*

Let's get right to it — the Big Question. Pregnant women think about it all the time but are too embarrassed to ask their doctors' advice. This concerns the delicate matter of whether or not it's safe for a woman to have sex during her pregnancy. You must understand that some doctors are extremely dense, and will advise her that sex is only safe when it's limited to her husband. But they will be happy to give you the following advice on your limitations:

1. It's a proven statistic that four out of five expectant fathers prefer the level of passion from an inflatable doll over what you're able to generate.

2. The wife should not attempt assuming the superior position during lovemaking for the last three months of pregnancy ... unless the husband is proficient in bench pressing Sherman tanks.

3. Be inventive. Try role playing games to inject some excitement into your sex lives. "Captain Ahab harpoons Moby Dick" is a real pleaser. Another popular one is the classic "Sir Edmund Hilary conquers Mt. Everest."

4. Use the sexual aid of fantasy. You pretend he's Tom Selleck, and he pretends you're NOT PREGNANT.

5. During the last two weeks of pregnancy, you must abstain totally from sex. If your husband complains that he can't stand it any longer and tries to woo you with romantic talk like "Fly with me down the runway of love," tell him to go on "manual-pilot" and take the controls in his own hands.

* * *

And, the delicate matter of when to resume marital relations after the baby is born has yet to be honestly addressed. It's a real problem because your sex drives are at vastly different levels. The husband is in the "clinical state" which can be medically described as — *Sex Starved.* The woman, on the other hand, has to contend with a whole new set of physical and mental problems brought on by childbirth. In the final analysis, the resumption of sexual relations is a highly personal choice depending on one's own natural inclinations. However, we hope that he will be reasonable and at least be willing to wait:

1. Until you have returned to the recovery room.

2. A few days until you heal. Men will never be able to understand the level of excruciating pain we have to endure which is associated with the "first time" post-partum. Most of them assume you're screaming because it feels so good. Dreading this event, many women choose to load up on prescription painkillers. But remember how fast acting these drugs can be. So to

spare his masculine ego, at least try to jump around a little and act excited before they take effect and you go totally numb or slip into unconsciousness after the first two minutes of foreplay.

3. Until the doctor has completed the removal of your 235 episiotomy stitches OR six months — whichever comes *last.*

4. Until your husband has completely recovered from the incredible grisly sights he was subjected to in the delivery room. (Warning: this could take up to several years.) Remember he has just witnessed, in technicolor, parts of the female anatomy which were, heretofore, seen only as black and white photographs in the back of some obscure textbook. He has just learned more about you than he really needed to know.

It's a well-known fact that a lactating mother's body will produce specific hormones which suppress the capability of conception for the period while she's breast feeding. This is nature's way of protecting the newborn's food source plus allowing sufficient time for the mother's body to restore itself. What is not so well known, is the theory that the body also secretes a complex of sex drive inhibiting hormones which act directly on the brain to accomplish the same thing. This phenomenon officially constitutes us as a "Hormonally Protected Species" and also accounts for the best sex evading excuses ever formulated:

"Not tonight, dear. My hormones are killing me."

"Not now, honey. The baby might be watching us."

"I'll be there as soon as I finish teaching the baby how to read."

"Would you mind starting without me?"

"Just a minute, sweetie. I have to finish expressing my last eight gallons of breast milk."

"Well, if YOU think I'm strong enough ... okay. But I can't keep my oxygen mask off for too long."

"Okay, darling. But keep in mind that my 300 razor sharp steel episiotomy sutures haven't been removed yet."

It's a good idea to hide this book from your husbands. We wouldn't want to give away any trade secrets now, would we? That dork Darwin missed the whole point. The female of the species has evolved highly because of our superior ability to think fast on our *backs* as well as on our feet. This is what we women call "Survival of the Slickest."

PART III QUIZ

1. Deep breathing is essential to a successful:
   a. X-Rated movie
   b. final stage of labor
   c. game of tongue hockey
   d. obscene phone call

   *d (especially if you're making it during b)

2. Another name for the amniotic sac is:
   a. Bag of Waters
   b. John Waters
   c. Hefty Cinch Sac
   d. Fruit of the Womb

   *c (guaranteed to hold up to 30 gallons without breaking)

3. A "Pit Drip" is most commonly used:
   a. at the Indy 500
   b. with a coffee maker
   c. with a dress shield
   d. none of the above

   *d (everyone knows a Pit Drip is a vicious breed of dog)

4. "Transition" identifies the stage of labor between:
   a. the agony and the ecstasy
   b. the good, the bad, and the ugly
   c. the devil and the deep blue sea
   d. 10 centimeters and blast off

   *b (respectively, this refers to the labor room nurse, your O.B., and you)

5.   An effective anesthetic for the actual delivery is:
   a. coma
   b. a speech by Dan Quayle
   c. napalm
   d. Midol

   *d (but only if free-based)

6.   Which is the best educational film for expectant women:
   a. Debbie Does Delivery
   b. Ernest Goes Through Delivery
   c. Delivering Miss Daisy
   d. Deliverance

   *c (conceived and filmed in the back seat of a 1950 Hudson)

7.   Which song best describes the experience of labor and delivery:
   a. "I Haven't Got Time For The Pain"
   b. "Breathless"
   c. "The Thrill Is Gone"
   d. "Sixteen Tons"

   *d (c refers to your sex life afterwards)

8.   Sex during pregnancy can be awkward if:
   a. you both try to be on top
   b. your husband comes home during it
   c. you are trying to do it between contractions
   d. you try to perform the same chandelier stunts that got you pregnant

   * you decide

9. After the baby is born, 9 out of 10 couples resume sex:
    a. without the other
    b. within the decade
    c. with someone else
    d. within a week after getting their tubes tied

    *c & d (with someone else within a week after getting their tubes tied)

10. The only safe condoms are:
    a. steel-belted
    b. ones having a strict tenant code
    c. lubricated with Super-Glue
    d. those worn by eunuchs

    * none of the above (the only *safe* condom is one in an unopened package)

11. The most beautiful thing about a pregnant woman is her:
    a. size 38 DD breasts
    b. healthy and shining coat
    c. strength and grace of a Clydesdale
    d. ability to provide adequate shade on a hot day

    *c (and cute "saddlebags" too)

12. When a woman is trying to conceive, the most helpful medical aid she can buy is:
    a. spermicide
    b. a young stud intern
    c. prayer beads
    d. the entire male hospital staff (for backup)

    *a (or any other FDA approved contraceptive will virtually guarantee conception)

PART IV

WOMEN UNDER THE KNIFE

Chapter 10

THE FACE-LIFT:

Stretching The Point

MYTH: *As long as you stay out of the sun, you'll never get wrinkles.*

Let's eavesdrop on a situation which is every woman's potential nightmare. You and your husband are sitting in an elegant restaurant celebrating your 15th wedding anniversary. The tuxedoed waiter takes your husband's order first and says to him: "Sir, and what will your mother be having?"

No question about it. After 40, the lack of youth-preserving hormones that keep the skin tight and glowing will result in the transformation of your face from a Georgia Peach into a California Raisin. When this happens, it's time to pack up those bags under your eyes and run to your nearest cosmetic surgeon. Here's what to expect:

THE CONSULTATION

Plastic surgeons are considered the "class acts" of medicine. You won't find them doing business out of any smelly old offices done up in '50s Sears decor. We're talking Mario Buatta suites fashioned from polished cotton chintzes and silk moiré. These fabrics produce the desired effect of "old money" — and Mario's suites positively reek of it. Even the office staff is dressed in designer uniforms made only from natural fabrics. They have their offices checked regularly by the EPA to detect the presence of any contaminating polyester fibers which would pollute the carefully controlled atmosphere. Plastic surgeons will go to such lengths in projecting a chic image that even their surgical smocks are supplied by Georgio Armani. And everyone's make-up is done to perfection — including the doctor's. No Tammy Faye faces here!

Cosmetic surgeons, as a rule, possess a slick demeanor as well as classy names — like Dr. Philip Flawless, whom we shall be discussing. Flawless, like all reconstructive surgeons, is extremely careful to avoid accurate descriptions like "wrinkled as a prune" or "old hag". Instead, he carefully chooses phrases like "redundant skin" and "mature dermis." These buzz words have track records longer than Secretariat for being money-makers. Be prepared to come with cash, too. Guys like Flawless get nauseous upon hearing words like "insurance" and "Medicare."

Besides never having to say he's sorry, Phil has built his practice around never saying what he means. So the conversation will probably go something like this:

"I am carefully retracting this small amount of redundant skin around your eyes to create the effect the surgery will achieve."

> TRANSLATION: "Boy, after hacking away at this bundle of flesh, there will be enough left over to graft John Candy's body — twice!"

Then he will smooth down the six layers of turkey wattle draping from your neck and push them back behind your ears, remarking: "At this juncture, we will be able to excise these folds and tack them, inconspicuously, behind the ears."

> TRANSLATION: "I'll have to call U.S. Steel for surgical cable strong enough to keep this mess suspended."

81

"And finally, this slightly puffy fatty tissue under the eyes can be removed. By concealing the stitches made in the natural crease below the lid, they will be virtually invisible when healed."

> TRANSLATION: "Gimme a break, woman. There are enough bags under here to pack for the entire *Pepsi Generation.*"

"You will be thrilled with the result. Of course, you can't realistically expect to look 20 years younger. But you will look rested — like you've been on a long vacation."

> TRANSLATION: "Who do you think I am — Doug Henning? With a little luck you might look 59 instead of 60."

Flawless will insist he'll get great results in about four hours of surgery. Carefully omitting any reference to the word "pain", he says, "You can expect 'mild discomfort' for the first 48 hours followed by some *nominal* swelling and bruising."

> TRANSLATION: "Your head will bloat up like a watermelon, and your face will look like you went 15 rounds with Mike Tyson."

THE RECOVERY ROOM

Only two words will insure survival here: *No Mirrors!* There's nothing which can ever prepare you for the shock of seeing your bandaged head, swollen to three times its normal size, sitting on top of a pair of tiny little shoulders. Jabba the Hut with a monstrous hangover is what you'll be seeing in your mirror. And bloodshot is the understatement of the year when you get a look at those eyes. You could tap enough blood from them to keep a blood bank in business for a month. Your friends will all ask the same question with great delicacy:

"Who on earth came after you with a baseball bat?"

After you explain about the surgery, some will say hesitatingly, you look "pretty good ... considering" .... But the honest ones will cover their eyes and run out of the room shrieking.

THE POST-OP UNVEILING

On the third day after surgery, the doctor will want to see you in his office. He will request that you enter through the back door, citing some phony excuse about the front door having been painted. The real reason is so you won't scare off his new patients in the waiting room who are sitting out there trying to decide whether or not to go through with it. Besides, the double doors in the rear are the only ones with enough clearance to allow your pumpkin-sized head to get through.

The first set of stitches to be removed are those which follow the contour of the ears up into the hairline. Looking in the mirror, you may note that you are now bearing a slight resemblance to Elsa Lanchester, as she appeared in the "Bride of Frankenstein." Not to worry. As each successive phase of suture removal progresses, this image will change into Gloria Swanson in "Sunset Boulevard," followed by Bette Davis in "Whatever Happened to Baby Jane?"

Before you leave, Flawless will issue lists of instructions longer than the Trump prenuptial agreement. Here's just a few of them:

1. Don't smoke.

2. Don't go out in the sun naked.

3. If you do, wear a 23 SPF sunblock at all times.

4. Don't sleep without elevating your head.

5. Don't sleep in an elevator.

6. Don't admit your true age to anyone.

7. Pay your bill on time.

8. Pay it in cash.

9. Don't try to save money by removing your own stitches.

10. Avoid looking in the mirror, except at the Fun House.

In the final analysis, your new lifestyle will leave you dead from boredom within three months, but you'll look ten years younger at the funeral.

After having cosmetic surgery. you're going to be the target of very pointed criticism from militant feminists, who will insist that plastic surgery does nothing to improve the image of women, already portrayed as frivolous and vain. They will insist that you should be spending your time supporting important issues like improving the environment.

Gently remind them that you ARE doing your part to keep America beautiful. Then advise them that they AREN'T, and on behalf of sisters everywhere, hand them your plastic surgeon's card.

There remains one unanswered question about this procedure which crosses every woman's mind. Because the life expectancy of a face-lift is about seven to ten years at best, if we keep having it done, will our ears meet after the third time? The answer is simple. Who wants to reach the age of 50 and look like Yoda? When our hormones let us down, it's our duty to lift our faces off the floor with a few well-placed stitches. Every woman wants to put her best face forward — especially if it is a different one every few years.

"SAY WHEN."

Chapter 11
THE BOOB JOB:
Keeping Up With Inflation

MYTH: *If God had intended for you to be a 36C, he would have made you that way.*

Women are the biggest liars in the world when they tell you they are having their breasts enlarged... *"because I want to do it for myself, not for men, just for ME."* Get serious! Every woman on the planet knows that big breasts mean power. And those who boast "My husband loves my 28 AAA breasts; he says he wouldn't want me any other way" are talking about a man who is obviously visually impaired. Let's face it. To a man's way of thinking, the bigger the better. If men had the option to have the organ of their choice augmented, they would all end up having to wear specially constructed jock straps to support the giant Sequoia in their pants.

So if you are among the many females who feel you were dealt a bad hand by nature and were given only enough hormones to grow two tiny ant hills on your chest, do something about it. Admitting the problem is the first step in finding a cure. Yes, say it. Repeat after me:

"I want a pair of totally bodacious ta-ta's which will make every man on earth stop dead in his tracks and drool over them."

Now — don't you feel better? The next step is to go out and find a good plastic surgeon.

But you need to be careful when choosing a plastic surgeon for breast augmentation surgery. Like any other profession, medicine is not exempt from having it's share of male chauvinists who won't take your needs seriously. You should have second thoughts about any surgeon who, during the consultation, refers to your breasts in any of the following terms:

— Boobs

— Jugs

— Knockers

— Headlights

— Zammers

— Tits or titties

— Bazooms

— Puppies

— Gazungas

Once you choose your doctor, he will want to discuss the size and kind of prosthesis available to you. The newer ones are filled with a gel, having the texture and consistency very close to real breast tissue. Years ago silicone was used. However it tended to become so dense and unyielding with age that thousands of husbands were injured in darkened bedrooms when they mistakenly entered into foreplay with bedposts.

After being injected into specific bodily locations, silicone had the added problem of "moving" from its original site. This caused a number of disgruntled husbands to file malpractice suits after finding their wives' breasts miles from home, often in strange bedrooms.

Today's models are a lot better. They can be filled with a saline solution or even inflated with air. But you will have to watch out for side effects like sudden blowout; or if they're overinflated, the potential of becoming airborne.

Use your good consumer sense, too, and don't accept those *factory seconds* implants offered by bargain outlets. Those cheaper prostheses are often filled with inferior materials to cut costs. So beware of sleazy salesmen who talk about the "rising cost of inflatables" while offering "cut rate" prices on their prostheses filled with "New Age" materials. The tip off will be in the bogus sales pitch touting the merits of:

GOOSEFEATHERS— "When you're going 'down' remember us."

SILLY PUTTY— "Put a handful of fun in your bra."

HELIUM— "It makes you feel like you're floating on air."

JELLO— "Watch 'em wiggle, see 'em jiggle."

LYCRA— (the *memory* fabric) "They stretch clear across the room then pop back for more!"

Size is important, too. Should you "go for it" and opt for the 36DD or stay with the more conservative 36B? Or compromise by getting one of each? How will you know when "enough" becomes "too much"? Well, if any of these things apply to you after the surgery, you'll really be calling yourself a *big boob:*

THE PENCIL TEST

Place an ordinary pencil under the breast. If it falls out when you raise your arms, then the prosthesis is the proper size and not too pendulous. However, once you surpass a gross and it's still holding them in there, remedial action should be taken.

SUPPORT BRA

When a 42DD bra molded from bulletproof Tupperware isn't giving you enough support, breasts of this size can be officially classified as "Hooters." You would automatically be considered a "bimbo" and offered a photo opportunity in "Playboy."

THE HINDENBURG FACTOR

Breasts filled with helium that approximate the size of a blimp should automatically carry a warning label. If you engage in any amount of rigorous foreplay, your husband / gigolo / significant other stands an increased risk of being killed from asphyxiation or possibly having his vocal pitch rise two octaves above normal. The worst case scenario is that you could be charged with the lesser crime of assault with a blunt, surgically manufactured, and overinflated weapon.

On the other hand, you don't want them so small that there's nothing to show "up front" for all your trouble and expense. No woman wants to suffer any of these humiliations at her gala unveiling:

- Your friends enlisting the aid of a magnifying glass to inspect them

- Being hounded by a bunch of attorneys who all want to file a malpractice suit on your behalf

- Watching your disappointed husband wandering around weeping on your friends' shoulders

- Snickers, titters, or all-out wild guffaws

- Your friends doing so many doubletakes, they go home with whiplashes

Having big breasts will give you a new slant on life. Literally. Besides listing forward at a 35° angle, you'll become the "life of the party" by delighting friends and family with an array of stunts you only dared fantasize about before:

- Floating in the hot tub without sinking

- Playing chopsticks on the piano without letting your hands touch the keyboard

- Balancing two martini glasses on both boobs

- Lying on your back and not having your boobs disappear into your armpits

- Doing the tango with a short guy and knocking him out cold on the turns

Come on! Do it! Isn't it time you took the Kleenex out of your bra and stopped using band-aids as a strapless? You owe it to yourself and your husband / boyfriend. And the person you'll owe the

MOST to? The surgeon, of course ... and he'll take it in cash.

Women who put themselves through all this trouble, time, and money are certainly not doing it just to please *themselves*. Would you pay $5,000 for a matching set of anything and keep it under wraps? You can have a lot of fun and be subtle about it, too. Next time you are out playing cards it would be entirely proper to draw attention to yourself by placing your hand next to your bosom and announcing, "Look here, everyone — I've got a perfect pair." Or host a charity auction where you can discreetly hold up some candlesticks in front of your décollatage and ask, "Who would like to bid on this gorgeous set?"

So don't let a lack of hormones keep your mammaries in an arrested state of development. Get a little help from your plastic surgeon and make mountains out of those molehills. And after you get it — don't forget to flaunt it!

"NURSE, CANCEL THE REST OF MY
APPOINTMENTS FOR THIS WEEK."

Chapter 12

SURGERY IS H.E.L.L.:

Hysterectomy — Electrolysis — Liposuction (and more Liposuction)

MYTH: *Good old-fashioned diet and exercise will get rid of those saddlebags around your hips.*

It's time for the sobering realization that there is no such thing as "natural beauty." This concept went out with the Grateful Dead concerts and love beads of the sixties. Nowadays, being beautiful "inside" and "out" is sheer illusion created by multiple cosmetic surgeries. Chances are, a gorgeous woman is shapely on the outside from liposuction, her skin is silky smooth from electrolysis treatments, and she is empty on the inside from a hysterectomy. And why not? Any woman who looks in a mirror would rather see a "surgical beauty" staring back at her than a "natural beauty" complete with saddlebags and a hormonally induced mustache.

LIPOSUCTION

For years scientists have been trying to isolate the gene responsible for saddlebags. However just when they get close, it gallops away. So the only other alternative is to get rid of the fat by liposuction. This is another one of those procedures which doctors love to label as "simple and painless." Well, if you think being knocked out cold under general anesthesia and attacked with a powerful Hoover qualifies as "simple and painless," then you need brain surgery, too. Actually, the worst part of this procedure is just prior to surgery, when the patient has to stand in the operating room, buck naked, and be publicly road-mapped with a surgical magic marker delineating the fatty areas to be lipo-sucked.

Most of these surgeries are humanely done under a general anesthetic, but if your surgeon decides a local will suffice, do yourself a big favor and bribe the anesthesiologist with an extra $50 for the "big sleep." Trust me. You don't want to be awake for this operation. You'd be subjected to less blood and violence if a butcher shop exploded.

The surgeon will make several incisions, placing the cannula, or fat-sucking nozzle, under the skin. Then, voilá! All those Ho-Ho's, Twinkies, and Dove Bars which have bypassed your stomach and were deposited directly on your hips and thighs over the years are sucked away. Some surgeons like to transfer the lipo-sucked fat from one part of the body to another area lacking in fat; for example, from the hips to the lips. Although it can produce the desired aesthetic effect, it's something you wouldn't want too many people to find out about. A guy might become slightly squeamish about kissing you if he knew he was actually kissing your butt.

The tragedy of fatty tissue, or "cellulite," is that it just won't go away. You can diet, roller pin it, or exercise to the point of Danskin burnout, but the cellulite remains. It can be found in all sorts of strange places, too — like on the kneecaps or in the ankles — and especially in all Loehmann's dressing rooms across the country. What woman doesn't despise the sight of those ugly little lumps of fat that bulge out under a sleeveless dress? They look like an extra set of training boobs. And what tummy, at one time or another, hasn't been responsible for cutting the lifespan of a 24 hour girdle down to 10 minutes? And something has to be done about this nationwide problem of under-arm jiggle. It's becoming so prevalent, that it's featured at least twice a week on Oprah.

We do not want to reach middle age looking like an undulating bag of Jello. We of the over 40 set need to entrust our bodies to a competent plastic surgeon. Find one who is board certified in lipo-suction. This means he has passed a rigorous exam given by a national board of Eureka sales-men. Once certified, he will be allowed to go door to door and take up great chunks of your precious time demonstrating liposuction techniques and cleaning your carpets at the same time.

The recovery period after liposuction varies according to how much fat tissue was removed. If it was just a few grams off the knees, allow about 24 hours of recovery time with your legs elevated. However, if you're going for a total body resculp-turing, the surgeon will have to hose out more blubber than your average Alaskan harpoons in a year. You'll be bandaged from head to toe and won't be doing much more than lying in state for about a week.

By and large, most women are very pleased with the results. The good news is, due to the short recovery period, you will soon *feel* like your old self again. The bad news is that if you gain any weight, you'll *look* like your old self again.

ELECTROLYSIS

Someone needs to hold a vigil for the old one-piece bathing suit with the pleated skirt. It has been officially put on the endangered species list. Nowadays, the most modest style available is one slit from the crotch to the armpits. And, it takes a special woman to wear these suits — a woman possessing two rare qualities — Anorexia and Total Absence of Body Hair. You know — that high fashion model type who is so skinny, even a pencil has more curves — and more body hair! Since this automatically rules out 99% of the population, we are forced to turn to our trusted Electrolysis Person for help. This profession is built around its promise of "painless hair removal." In your dreams! The only way this is going to happen is to show up for your appointment packing a combo of Percodan, Demerol, and Novocaine.

Electrolysis is accomplished with the use of an electric needle. We all know that zapping out an over-grown female mustache or goatee doesn't require the skill of a DeBakey, but the operator must be competent, at the very least. When you get down around the "bikini" area, a slip of the hand could mean the difference between your putting on a bathing suit or the first female Bris.

HYSTERECTOMY

This operation is now considered one of the most frequently performed "unnecessary surgeries." Are doctors just out for the bucks? Unfortunately, a woman must be knowledgeable enough to answer this question for herself. To identify these knife-happy gynecologists, be on the lookout for those who insist a hysterectomy is medically indicated:

1. While you're still on the table after delivering your first child.

2. When your supply of tampons runs out.

3. As a 40th birthday present to yourself.

4. The week before their malpractice insurance bill is due.

5. To fill up his morning's surgical schedule.

The jury is still out on this operation, and with enough bribes from the AMA, they won't be back either. But, there are a lot of myths surrounding hysterectomy which have been exposed beyond a reasonable doubt as purely old wives' tales:

1. "After a hysterectomy I'll only be half a woman." *Totally false. You'll be* $^2/_3$ *to* $^3/_4$ *depending on how much was removed.*

2. "Sex won't be the same after the operation." *Nonsense. It will continue to be every bit as dull and boring as before.*

3. "I'll be filled with *remorse* after I do it." *No way. You'll be filled with **gas** — and enough to launch the Goodyear Blimp!*

4. "I will lose my driving urge for sex." *Not exactly. Your preference will simply switch to the back seat.*

5. "Losing my female organs will be a constant reminder that I'm hollow inside." *Untrue. You'll only echo if somebody shouts directly into your cervix.*

Women are constantly seeking answers as to what goes wrong with the uterus to warrant a hysterectomy. The answer — what else? *Hormones.* If you're producing too much or too little estrogen, your natural secretions diminish. The cure? A lube job. Sometimes the ligaments holding the uterus in place lose their muscle tone, and it begins to slip downwards. How can you tell if this happens? You'll be tripping a lot. The cure? A suspension job. Your gynecologist will be happy to do any of these procedures for you, but many women prefer to take bids by local construction companies. They can get a better deal — plus a 5-year warranty on parts and labor.

Personally, it really irritates me to listen to women actually bragging about what great shape their reproductive organs are in. How many times have you heard some pinhead boasting, "My doctor says I have perfect plumbing." It just makes you want to reply "Oh yeah, what do you do — douche with Drano?" That ought to shut her up.

Doctors keep telling us that if we have a hysterectomy, we will rid ourselves of the constant pain and discomfort associated with female problems. So we check into the hospital, have the surgery, and wake up in pain worse than labor which lasts for three unrelenting days. But we are assured by the doctor that at long last our problems are over. What they forget to tell you is that you'll be needing additional hormone therapy!! We have to replace the hormones we are no longer producing. If you take too much of one, you wake up with a beard and chest hair. So you take more of another and end up growing auxiliary breasts. Then you're having multiple hot flashes from too little estrogen. The truth is you'll be spending the rest of your life feeling like a man trapped in the body of a woman trapped in the body of a man. What should you do about it? You can always go on Donahue.

There's just too big an emphasis placed on reproductive organs when 99% of the time they're not used for reproducing anyway. The inevitable had to happen. Technology is slowly replacing our female organs one by one. The uterus has already become obsolete ... it's been replaced by the test tube.

PART IV QUIZ

1. Never use a plastic surgeon who:
   a. flashes his money
   b. flashes your money
   c. flashes a badge
   d. is a flasher

   *c (the *bust* he's trying to make is not the one you're looking for)

2. Following a facelift, if you are unable to smile for six months it means:
   a. the surgeon charged too much
   b. the surgeon didn't charge enough
   c. the corners of your mouth are touching the tips of your ears
   d. you'll need further surgery

   *d (this time for hemorrhoids)

3. Following a facelift you can expect to look:
   a. one year younger
   b. straight ahead for a few months
   c. for Demerol
   d. for one year younger guys

   * if a is true then go for d

4. A good place to appear inconspicuous after a facelift is:
   a. a boxing ring
   b. Madame Tussaud's Wax Museum
   c. at a mummy's tomb
   d. at a "Battered Wives" Ball

   *d (Black Eye optional)

5. When considering breast augmentation surgery, your husband says SIZE doesn't matter. Tell him:

    a. it does in HIS case
    b. it will double your pleasure, double his fun
    c. he's cute when he lies
    d. to get a seeing-eye dog

    *a (then recommend he get penile augmentation for himself)

6. A breast prosthesis is inappropriate if:

    a. it's wearing the K-Mart label
    b. it can double as a wooden leg
    c. it requires frequent refills with a service station air hose
    d. it's not sold as part of a set

    *d (and make sure they're both the same size)

7. To make sure people will notice your newly enlarged bust at a party:

    a. wear a flashing neon bra
    b. pass them around at the party
    c. don't remove the price tag while wearing them
    d. display them on the salad bar next to the deviled eggs

    * all of the above seem like reasonable conversation pieces

8. Your breast augmentation surgery is covered by:
   a. Medicare
   b. Blue Cross-Your-Heart
   c. Jimmy the Greek
   d. Geraldo Rivera

   *d (Geraldo's presentations are all *busts*)

9. Removing fat from an unsightly place is best achieved by:
   a. liposuction
   b. lip-syncing
   c. lipreading
   d. kicking your husband out of his favorite bar

   *a (Note: but does not work for fat-headedness)

10. In today's society, "underarm flab" is:
    a. grounds for divorce
    b. correctable with a special truss
    c. a good cause for a telethon
    d. something channeled by Shirley MacLaine

    *c (Jerry Lewis already bought the rights to it)

11. A uterine growth the size of a tennis ball is:
    a. called a Navratilovarian cyst
    b. called a Graffian follicle
    c. the chief cause of Vitasgerulitis
    d. André Agassi Jr.

    *d (if you're a tennis groupie and have been hanging around his hotel room a lot)

12. Blocked Fallopian tubes can best be relieved by:
    a. All-Bran
    b. Liquid Plumber
    c. Roto-Rooter
    d. dynamite

  *c (but only if a plunger fails to work)

PART V
THE LIBIDO
IN LIMBO

THE ONLY *100% SAFE* CONTRACEPTION

Chapter 13

CONTRACEPTION:

I'm Just A Girl Who Can't Say No

MYTH: *The technology of birth control has made quantum leaps into the Space Age.*

Who are we kidding? It's the end of the 20th century, and birth control practices are still in the Stone Age. And what's worse, many new products on the market still pose major health risks — and, of course, all to women. We need to make the 21st century an epoch where birth control becomes the Sole Responsibility of the Male. C'mon, we women have got a lot more to do than sit around thinking about spermicides all day. The thought of all those desperate sperm getting killed is just too big a guilt trip for us to handle.

After considering the options available to us, intelligent women should use the only 100% safe *oral* birth control: the word "No." And if that's just not possible, here are a few of the prehistoric birth control methods still available to us:

THE IUD

Do you remember reading about the torture racks popular during the Spanish Inquisition? Well, like the kid in "Poltergeist II" says, "They're BAAAACK." And you can find them installed in your gynecologists' offices. Everyday, women are stretched out on them and "fitted" with their IUD's. Note: the term "fitted" is used loosely here. Constructed of serrated steel and displaying several rows of tooth-like structures die cast from Jaws models, they act like a charm to lure unsuspecting sperm to their grisly demise. There is a basic problem, though. To place one in the uterus, the IUD with its one inch diameter must be forced through a $1/2$-inch opening of the cervix. And to compound things, most gynecologists insist they are dexterous

110

enough to insert them without anesthesia. Oh sure! And these are the same guys who won't clip their own toenails without having a sedative first.

And how do they fare for safety? Let us count the lawsuits. Most pharmaceutical companies employ men who go to great lengths in playing down their risks. Male doctors are also a part of this conspiracy. Do you realize the little pat speech they spout about the safety and reliability of the IUD was written by a team of used car salesmen?

> "Now, ladies. We do not pretend to gloss over some minor risks here. But infection, hemorrhage, death ... we're talking peanuts in exchange for the happiness of a husband who won't have to use those miserable condoms anymore."

It seems to me that the equitable solution to this problem is for an all-female pharmaceutical company to devise a male counterpart of the IUD. It would be "painlessly" inserted into the male's urethra via a Foley catheter. And since it would be inserted only four inches into the urethra, according to what you men have told us about your personal anatomical structures, you could easily accommodate it with an extra two to six inches to spare. So come on, guys. Help us gals with this birth control thing by giving your "fair share". We're sure you can all rise to meet the operation.

THE DIAPHRAGM

Inserting one of these things requires the dexterity of a seasoned magician like David Copperfield. You might even want to ask David to help you, but chances are he's booked already. The mere THOUGHT of having to insert a diaphragm sends many women off packing to the Convent. Most people don't realize that the diaphragm is manufactured by the same company who makes the Frisbee. Constructed of latex rubber with a spring action stronger than a mousetrap's, extreme caution should be taken when trying to insert it. Letting it slip before it's halfway in could result in the diaphragm shooting across the room and slicing your ficus tree in half. The worst part is reaching your hand into what feels like a Giant Clam — a sensation about as pleasant as feeling dead fish. Probing along, your goal is to find the tip of the cervix. Once you're there (it seems like about 30 feet), your elbow may have disappeared. Now it's time to let go of the diaphragm's spring action, allowing it to snap into the correct position. Brace yourself against a wall because when you let go, the uterus will be absorbing shock waves of an intensity not felt since Hiroshima.

Physicians say the diaphragm has a high success rate of preventing pregnancy when used properly. Also, it must be removed within 12 hours after sexual relations. The bad news is that getting it OUT makes putting it IN look like child's play. You have to go through all those *pleasant* sensations you did when inserting it, PLUS now you have to hook your finger around its delicate rim, greased up by the repeated applications of spermicidal jelly. A note of caution: fingernails are the diaphragm's biggest enemy. You can very easily tear through the fragile latex with a well-manicured talon. And for heaven sakes, don't go after it wearing Lee press-on nails. Women have been known to lose an entire set of them and still fail to remove the diaphragm. This is also nearly, if not downright impossible, to explain to a gynecologist. It's more embarrassing than having your gynecologist try to retrieve your tampon because you lost the string during insertion. At least they see that in their practice all the time — like about 1,000 yards of tampon string a year.

FOAM

In order to be effective, contraceptive foam has to be used in the same quantities it would take to cover a runway for an emergency landing of a Boeing 747. One of the biggest drawbacks of foam is that swimming is prohibited for 24 hours after application, because the user now has the dangerous potential of acting as a giant Alka-Seltzer tablet.

JELLIES

Similar to the principle of foam, this stuff can be far more hazardous to both sexes. If left in place too long, it can "set-up," with the potential of becoming harder than a rock. Then, when attempting any future sexual activity, penetration will be almost impossible unless the male uses a condom with a tiny miner's helmet on the end. And he must be made aware of the very real possibility of suffering mutilation in a mine shaft collapse.

THE SPONGE

This is a new and unique idea in contraceptive items. It is small, compact, and has earned millions for the O-Cello Company. Appearing to be the safest product to come along in years, it does have one side effect — not dangerous, but annoying. Once it's in place, the wearer is cautioned that upon entering the bathtub, the water level will become drastically reduced. Head injury must also be mentioned as a rare, but possible side effect from making sudden moves while wearing the sponge. For example, carelessly flopping into a chair might create a "rebound" effect, catapulting one headfirst into the ceiling.

THE PILL

Who needs it? The package alone contains more warnings than were issued at the Iran/Contra Hearings. Some of the possible side effects include stroke, heart attack, cancer, unwanted pregnancy, and divorce. Plus, if you smoke, the incidences are all doubled. If you smoke and drink — triple it. If you smoke, drink, and have sex — forget it! You won't live long enough to finish out the package. Expert medical advice tells us that Russian Roulette gives better odds.

CONDOMS

The first complaint about this birth control product comes from the female sector of the population. We think the manufacturers need to design a package that takes less time to open. While all men still cling to the story that they can last for an entire evening, most of them can't even last until they get the package open. The second complaint is from the men themselves, who are concerned about the expiration date stamped on a box of condoms. They all say the same thing: "Who needs this kind of pressure?"

THE RHYTHM METHOD

This rarely works. And unless you're doing it with Bobby Brown in the room, forget it.

CELIBACY

It is a scientific fact that any organ which is not used regularly will eventually atrophy. For example, an idle brain will show signs of a lowered I.Q.; a leg rendered immobile by a cast will develop withered muscles, and teeth not subjected to the constant grinding of food will fall out. And an unused sex organ will do all of the above — and in the same order! This poses a double tragedy for some men, too, since their brains are reputedly located in their sex organs. So we all need to heed the old saying, "Use it or lose it."

The good news is that there IS one completely safe, painless, and trouble-free birth control solution available to 100% of the women everywhere. It's called VASECTOMY — and we're all for it!

* * *

In sum, contraception has always been and continues to be a big problem for women. And the hormonal mechanisms that interplay to produce an egg and provide it with the optimum environment for its development are incredibly powerful. At the time of ovulation, the female begins to produce further potent hormones, making her feel like she's in heat. And technically she is. Nature's drive to procreate hits a peak, creating an irresistible hormonal urge to mate immediately. So on one hand, you've got these hormones from hell saying, "Do it! Do it!" and on the other, your good sense saying, "Are you crazy? You're gonna get pregnant!" It's a dilemma worse than watching a "Geraldo vs. Satan" show and having to decide — who do you root for?

115

Chapter 14
SEX AFTER FORTY:
Mission Impossible

MYTH: *Sex gets BETTER after 40.*

Maybe for Jane Fonda, but for the rest of us, the following scene is the general rule:

The husband whines and complains bitterly: "Gee dear, I can't remember when the LAST time we had sex was."

The wife shoots back: "Oh yeah? Well I CAN and that's why we aren't having it anymore!"

But take heart. Sex after 40 doesn't have to become a memory. It simply means changing the game plan a little to make accommodations for a body that is going downhill faster than Jean Claude Killy. Women have to be on the alert for situations which have the potential for making their bodies appear in worse shape than they already are. We must pay attention to details like:

POSITION

After 40, a woman's main concern during sex is to display her body in the most flattering position available. This automatically eliminates the hope of ever assuming the superior role again during lovemaking, because it makes the face fall forward and just HANG there, jowls and all. This sight will take the starch out of the best of 'em. Also, laying flat out on one's back has the dangerous potential of quadrupling the square footage of thigh spread; a sight so grotesque, your partner may keep the sheet pulled up to your chin.

We women are convinced that scientists will soon be isolating the "cellulite gene" that produces the devastating hormone responsible for lumping up all our body fat. But until they do, we'll have to monitor our body positions carefully.

LIGHTING

The older we get, the less light we desire on the lovemaking scene. Remember in your 20's when you made love in broad daylight, on beaches, in cars, and in the shower? After 40, ladies, we've got a lot more to hide than just our crow's feet. Our bedrooms will slowly make the transition from 60-watt flood bulbs, to 40-watt, to a nightlight, then finally to about half the candlepower generated by an elderly firefly. By age 60, we're talking about a room so dark it can only be navigated by bats.

FOREPLAY

Do you remember that? He probably doesn't. Past 40, there is very little actual kissing going on in the bedroom. It takes too much time and saps too much of the energy necessary to complete the actual act. A common practice past 40 is for both partners to meet in the center of the bed, shake hands, and get on with it.

Young women foolishly spend all their time worrying about what kind of orgasm they are SUPPOSED to experience. The studies tell us all about the differences between the vaginal, clitoral, uterine, multiple, and most popular, the faked orgasm. But by 40, women aren't worried about having multiple orgasms anymore, they're worried about having multiple ORGANISMS. At our age, we're becoming more prone to bladder infections, worried about Monilia, Herpes, AIDS and many other sexually transmitted diseases. We can't help being neurotic. We're victims of our own dangerous sexual times. Men should never take it personally when a mature woman leaps out of bed just seconds after making love and stays in the bathroom douching with Commercial Strength Lysol till dawn.

LENGTH OF TIME

Face it, couples in their "mature" years simply do not have the staying power they had in their earlier days. Also, the stress associated with lengthy foreplay can pose a serious cardiac risk, and vigorous passionate clenches can mean curtains for a prolapsed bladder. Worse yet, lengthy orgasms can reduce blood flow to the brain resulting in the demoralizing situation where one partner has to ask the other, "Did we do it yet?"

SEX AFTER "THE CHANGE"

The change changes everything. The cessation of menstruation will cause a sharp reduction in the hormones which are necessary for the body to produce its normal amount of secretions and lubricants. To put it bluntly, we're talking about a physiological environment for sex drier than the Betty Ford Clinic. Sometimes the hormone level drops so low, it may be necessary to apply K-Y Jelly in generous quantities just to shake hands. After menopause, women will have the added problem of trying to differentiate a hormonal "hot flash" from the "hot and flushed" feeling signaling sexual arousal. And since you'll be experiencing hot flashes with increasing frequency, you may find yourself in a constant state of confusion. Not to mention how hard it is on your husband. He may find himself going up and down more times in one night than a hotel elevator.

Women who are experiencing a renewed interest in sex secretly fantasize about being in the ideal environment to make love which:

    1.   Brings no fear of pregnancy

2. Offers a variety of locations for the tryst
3. Has an element of danger in being caught
4. Offers a surplus of available partners

The good news is that this is all possible. Where? In an Old Folks Home. This has got to be the best kept secret on earth besides Elton John's sexual preference. But now the secret's out. Those seniors are having the time of their lives sneaking around from room to room, carrying on all hours of the day and night. According to all reports, they're logging more hours in the saddle than world class polo players and doing the posture-pedic polka well into the wee hours of the morning. What a great thing to look forward to. They always say to save the "best" for "last." And what a way to go!

Women believe in the old adage "Sex Is All In Your Mind." So when your hormones begin to betray you in your later years, get smart and start using the biggest sexual organ of all — your brain. The best stud brains in America have recently invented several ways for us to enjoy great technological sex without the need for a young supple body. We are all familiar with the group "Parents Without Partners." Well, now technology has enabled us to form a new sister chapter for menopausal women, called "Sex Without Partners." They have made it possible for us to enjoy solo activities like phone sex, computer sex, and battery-operated sex. For those who desire multiple partners, phone sex with *call waiting* is ideal. Computer generated sex is perfect for voyeurs who are heavy into graphic sex. And for the sexually motivated athletes, or self-starters, they can take part in solo events like the popular "Vibrator Olympics." So let the competition begin — *ladies, start your batteries!*

Chapter 15

NEW AGE SEX:

No-No's In The Nineties

MYTH: *A __good__ girl never sleeps with a man she isn't in love with.*

Living in the "New Age" doesn't necessarily mean it's not without its new problems. Even though we may be given more options and choices in our sexual behavior, we shouldn't sit around moping because we're past our sexual peaks. The truth is, it's a jungle out there in the land of the Sexually Active. Maybe we should be glad our hormonally-impaired reproductive organs are representing their own era, otherwise known as the Age of the Listless Libido.

In the New Age, people don't waste valuable time talking about love. They've got more potent sexually stimulating hormones coursing through them than Baskin-Robbin's has flavors. So they just settle for "know" — which means about a 30 minute conversation. During these days of the dangerous diseases, you'd better show up at your favorite pickup bar armed with a checklist twice as long as Gene Simmon's tongue. It's the best sexual aid you'll ever find to help in identifying potentially safe partners. Remember, you're already the victim of your own hormones, so you don't want to be the victim of somebody else's misguided ones. The keystone of the 90's is precaution — and Safe Sex doesn't mean "not falling off the bed" like it used to. So take along your checklist and make your opening line something like this:

"Hi there ... say ... you're kinda cute — but first, do you happen to have ... (at which point you pull out your list)

- Herpes I?
- Syphilis?
- Herpes II?
- AIDS?
- Herpes MDXXVIII?
- Genital Warts?
- Clap?
- Crabs?
- Gonorrhea?
- Cold Sores?
- Running Sores?
- Running Shoes (smelly)?
- Body Lice?
- Body Odor?
- Heart Disease?
- Heartworm?
- Facial tics?
- Dog ticks?
- Flat feet?
- Crows feet?
- The Heartbreak of Psoriasis?
- Ringworm?
- A pinkie ring?
- A chest hair dickey?
- Gold chains?
- A membership to the Hair Club for Men?"

Also, sexual identity can get pretty confusing in the New Age, so you've got to be sure the person you're contemplating doesn't throw you any surprises. The situation clearly warrants further cross-examination, employing the tough tactics last used during the McCarthy hearings:

"Well ... you sure look like a Major Hunk to me, big guy ... but ... are you now or have you ever been:

- Married or single?

- Straight or Gay?

- Bisexual or heterosexual?

- Jewish or Gentile?

- Transsexual or transvestite?

- Aphrodite or hermaphrodite?

- A cross-dresser or wearing a Cross-Your-Heart?

- Into leather, S&M, or Cool Whip?

- Featured in the chorus line of La Cage Aux Folles?

- A love child of Steve Garvey?

- In love with Steve Garvey?"

If you somehow make it past all those major hurdles and actually decide to "do it", the next step is to decide upon a mutually agreeable form of condom. This information must be finessed with as much dignity as possible under the circumstances. A genteel way of introducing the topic would be:

"Condom?"

"Don't mind if I do."

"Latex or sheepskin?

Standard or extra thin?

Colored or natural?

Ribbed or smooth?

Lubricated or non-lubricated?

Spermicide or plain?

Reservoir tipped or blunt end?

Designer or generic?

Jif or Skippy?

Battery powered or kick start?

French tickler or French vanilla?

Eelskin or sharkskin?

Forward or reverse gear?

Wesson oil or motor oil?

Sausage or Pepperoni stuffed?"

Whew! Now we're getting someplace. If all systems are go — then the next phase is choosing a mutually agreeable site and setting:

"Your place or mine?

Outdoors or indoors?

Back seat or front?

127

Waterbed or regular mattress?

Night time or nooner?

Candlelit or dark?

Bathtub or shower stall?

Video camera or Polaroid?

Naked or basic Victoria's Secret?

Straight or kinky?

Sexual aids or fantasy?

120 or 220 volt?

Orchestra pit or aisle?

Individual or group plan?

French or English horn?

Kiddie pool or steno pool?

Amyl nitrate or sodium nitrate?

Prison Warden or basic Nazi?

Will you be Batman or Robin?"

Holy Hormones! Once all the particulars have been worked out, unfortunately so has your sex urge. At this rate, "Zero Population Growth" is bound to become a self-fulfilling prophecy in the New Age.

Let's not forget that a lady *always* has the prerogative of changing her mind. In fact, most women change it more often than their vibrator batteries. And if the guys you date don't like it, too bad. To make your point, simply pull out a torn condom and shout — "Stop In The Name of Love!"

And if you think the dating scene is just too sexually demanding for your tastes, and you're afraid you might end up disappointing a lot of guys — get married — that way you'll only have to disappoint one.

PART V QUIZ

1. The Surgeon General recommends buying condoms at:
   a. a retread outlet
   b. Condoms 'R' Us
   c. 10.5%
   d. none of the above

   *d (wait until the rates come down to 9.75%)

2. When a diaphragm is inserted improperly:
   a. the voice is lowered 2 octaves
   b. you sprain 2 fingers
   c. breathing becomes difficult
   d. none of the above

   *d (all are associated with *normal* insertion)

3. An important factor in the success of the rhythm method is:
   a. Paula Abdul
   b. The Pope
   c. low IQ
   d. the music at Chippendales

   *c & d work effectively together

4. The most important element in foreplay is:
   a. an anti-climax
   b. a Tony Award performance
   c. a good stiff scotch
   d. a good stiff

   *b,c,d (without them you get <u>a</u>)

5. The most common type of orgasm experienced by women is:

   a. multiple
   b. faked
   c. Wurlitzer
   d. none when he's above

   *b (and 99.9% of the time)

6. Spermicide plus the sponge is a hazardous combination because it:

   a. can take the shine off your floors
   b. can bio-degrade your sex toys
   c. is flammable and can start bush fires
   d. can become habit forming

   *b (synthetic and *live*)

7. The G-Spot can be found:

   a. on the 5th fret of Eddie Van Halen's guitar
   b. somewhere in Dr. Ruth's bedroom
   c. on page 69 of the Hite Report
   d. somewhere on a G-Man

   *c (and has never been found anyplace else but here)

8. Genital warts are most commonly found in:

   a. consenting frogs
   b. the weekly plot lines of *thirtysomething*
   c. the PTL
   d. participating 7-11 stores

   *too close to call

9. Coitus interruptus is practiced by:
   a. attorneys
   b. Roman Catholics
   c. masochists
   d. all of the above

   *d (especially Roman Catholic masochist attorneys)

10. Who should be responsible for defective condoms:
   a. Marvin Mitchelson
   b. the parents of the bride
   c. the pharmacist
   d. the flea market vendor

   *c (if he put it on improperly)

11. Orgasm after 40 can be compared to:
   a. waiting for Godot
   b. your chances of winning the New York Lottery
   c. an Academy Award performance
   d. the statement "your check is in the mail"

   *c (if *Oscar* gives a great performance)

12. Pain during intercourse is a sign that:
   a. your instruction manual is upside down
   b. you are awake this time
   c. three's a crowd
   d. the steering wheel is too close

   *d (Rx: next time get a stretch limo)

EPILOGUE

Many of us are at the point in our lives when we will be sitting down with our daughters and giving them our modern day version of the "Big Talk." We'll be "grabbing 10" on our lunch hour from Merrill-Lynch, dressed in our business pinstripe Armani's with the "I Can Have It All" button displayed on the lapel. Smiling, we'll look down at those same innocent expectant faces like we used to have, and deliver our revised speech, chock full of present day attitude:

"Okay, Babe, let's make this quick. I'm on my lunch hour and the market's so bullish, I'll be knee-high in cow flops if I don't burn rubber and get back on the floor. So here's the deal on this menstrual thing, and I'm shootin' straight from the hip."

1. A young girl dreads the day she gets her period and hates it for the rest of her life. But that's okay, honey. It's perfectly normal to vent your feelings of hostility by slapping those sanitary pads around from time to time.

2. Every woman on the planet HATES going to the gynecologist. But this does not make the gynecologist a bad person. We need to think of him as a good person who's simply been put into a bad position. But remember, no matter how bad his position looks, yours will look worse when you get on the examination table.

3. A woman looks and feels like hell during pregnancy. But that doesn't mean she has to go through it alone. She needs to share this experience with a loving and understanding husband by her side, so she'll have someone to harass and abuse for nine months.

4. Natural childbirth is the most beautiful experience a woman can have — if her brain waves are the same frequency as a fern's.

5. Sex is still POSSIBLE after 40 — but only with a great deal of help from mail order items.

6. Small breasts are going to stay small no matter how many bust developers you order from Mark Eden. So don't waste your money or your hopes on him. The only thing Mark is going to develop is his assets. But women have choices nowadays. You can either learn to live with those micro-mamms or go out and find the best plastic surgeon in town.

"So, you think you've got the picture? Good! I've got to run now, babe. And if there's anything I missed in our discussion about sex, you can explain it to me when I get home."